I0006329

Forward

This book is dedicated to Bert Johnson, my wonderful, loving but non-computer savvy husband

The inspiration for this simple, little e-book came from my husband Bert. Once a month, without fail, he carries his Mac to me mournfully, as if it were a dead animal. On the screen is usually a blinking, flashing "Malware-as-a Service" site, demanding that you call a certain number and pay money, or your data will be forever locked away. At least this is the usual. Sometimes it is a different form of malware, but the result is always the same. I end up stopping what I am doing, disabling the malware, then tracing back what he was doing before the malware was accessed.

As the holder of a CISSP (Certified Information Security Specialist) certification, I know how to avoid these issues myself, and usually find that my poor non-computer savvy husband has made a typical error that I have warned him not to make. So, I give him "Cybersecurity Lecture" number 1xxx, and hope for the best in the future. But this is disruptive to my workflow, and potentially places our savings and worse, our identities, at risk.

We have a nice Mac for him at our main house, but to prevent carrying computers back and forth, we have an inexpensive PC at our condo which is doubly vulnerable to malware.

This time I told myself I was going to write a simple, easy to follow book and make sure he has it in front of him while working on his computer. That way I can just say "Page 26" instead of giving another lecture on cybersafety. It also occurred to me that other seniors may not live with someone who can restore their computers, and then lecture them on why it is so prudent to exercise safe surfing. And it is not just seniors who have issues with computers, I have other friends who avoid them like the plague and only use them when there is no other option.

Hence the birth of this little, easy to read and use guide to staying safe in our increasingly computerized, automated day and age! I hope it saves you (and whatever poor relative or friend fixes these things for you) tons of time, money, and frustration in the future. Thank you so much for buying my little book. If you enjoy it and it helps you, please tell your friends or write a review so others can benefit.

TABLE OF CONTENTS

Introduction

Hackers are not going away, folks. This is a sad but true fact of life. My husband keeps asking why they are allowed to get away with stuff like this. They are legion, so stopping the ones that go after consumers and individuals is kind of like eliminating all the ants from a woodpile – not gonna happen. The government is very busy trying to keep military secrets, banks, and corporate intellectual property safe from nation-state bad actors, disgruntled former employees, and hacktivists who think they are doing good deeds, so it is up to YOU to ensure the safety of your personal data and machines.

In today's world, we use our computers for most of our personal business. Banking, medical records, medical insurance communications etc. are just more convenient for the corporate entities than paper and mailings. Social security and disability reporting and applications are now mostly online. So as much as you may want to escape the cyberworld, eventually it will become a necessity in your life.

Cyberthieves count on this, and they LOVE non techies they can trick, cheat, abuse and rip off.

And the stakes are high. Although most malware is simply annoying by causing a temporary loss of use of your computer and possibly a lot of sirens and other noise through your speakers, some hackers go for your savings accounts. Even worse, many go for your very identity so they can bring criminals, prostitutes or even spies into this country. Identity theft is very real and not just the subject of box office movie smash hits. Reestablishing your identity once it has been stolen can be a long and arduous road if you don't have identity theft insurance. This is WHY the journey has made such compelling books and movies.

But YOU don't want to have your life resemble a movie, and you really don't want to be a victim to these unscrupulous people. You are in the right place, time to read on.

PART I: ID10T Errors

A joke that has been running on social media for some time goes like this...

"I was having trouble with my computer. So I called David, the 11 year old next door whose bedroom looks like Mission Control, and asked him to come over.

David clicked a couple of buttons and solved the problem.

As he was walking away, I called after him, "So, what was wrong?"

He replied, "It was an ID ten T error."

I didn't want to appear stupid, but nonetheless inquired, "An ID Ten T error?

What's that? In case I need to fix it again."

David grinned, "Haven't you ever heard of an ID ten T error before?"

"No", I replied.

"Write it down," he said, "and I think you'll figure it out."

So, I wrote down: I D 1 0 T

I used to like that little boy."

Nobody wants to hear they just made an ID10T error, yet most seniors didn't grow up with computers. Or at least with the types of computers we have today (some of us in our 60s had TRS-80s, affectionally known as "Trash" 80s from Radio Shack). Those of us in the tech industry were forced to keep up with the rapid changes that computers and software have experienced, but many in other lines of work were not expected to continuously adapt to the latest and greatest software or platform.

Many must rely on someone like me, or David the little boy. No, you are not an ID10T but can feel like one after a "dyed in the wool" techie resolves your issue in five minutes and goes back to his or her day. Keeping this book on your desk and following its guidance should help you ensure you don't have to face that kind of humiliation.

This section of our simple eBook is dedicated to the simple things, so you don't have to be told by a "little shit" that you made an ID10T error!

Chapter One: Passwords

The biggest ID10T error one can make is to use a password like "Password123". Or even worse, "Admin". "123456" and simply "password" qualifies as equally bad. Next is to use your first name and "123" after it. Yet another one is to use the same password for all your accounts and sign-ins; if the bad guys hack into one account, they've got them all.

"But", you may claim, "I HATE remembering all these crazy passwords and my memory is not as good as it used to be. I have to call the jerk next door every time I forget a password for help resetting it."

Don't worry, help is on the way. You can always get a physical password book and write each one down in it. Keep it in a place no one will think to look, like your bread box or underneath the sofa. If that is too much hassle, or like me, your handwriting is undecipherable, then an alternative is to use a program called 1Password. 1Password automatically generates strong passwords that look like an alien language, auto fills passwords for you into your browser, allows you to store everything in one location, and removes the need to memorize a bunch of passwords.

1Password uses something called "multilayer encryption" to keep your passwords safe, so all you must do is sign into your 1Password account and let it do the rest.

If you do opt for the notebook password storage method, I suggest making a copy of it and putting it into a safe or a safe deposit box. Otherwise, if you have a fire or other disaster, you will have to reset all your passwords and start over. And people do loot after a fire.

1Password is a program known as a "Password Manager" and is generally known as the best. Others include one from Google, Bitwarden, Keeper, Nordpass, LastPass and Dashlane. All these solutions take the burden of remembering all your passwords off you and provide an added layer of security. They cost varying amounts, but all are cheaper than the cost of identity theft.

Whether you opt for a Password Manager or a notebook, the important things to remember are to keep the password list safe, use different passwords for different sites, and use long, non-easily guessable passwords. ANY easily recognizable words in a password make it easier for hackers to use computer algorithms to reverse engineer your password. Random combos of numbers, special characters, and capital letters make it harder for them. Remember, your password should look like an alien language, NOT something that an algorithm can decipher in fifteen minutes.

Rules of thumb for good password creation are:

- **Length**: Make your passwords long. Aim for at least 12 characters and consider going even longer if the platform allows it.

- **Complexity**: Use a mix of uppercase and lowercase letters, numbers, and special characters. This makes it harder for attackers to guess or crack your password.

- **Avoid Dictionary Words**: Avoid using easily guessable words found in dictionaries. Instead, create a passphrase or string together unrelated words.

- **Unique Passwords**: Use unique passwords for each of your accounts. If one account gets compromised, having a unique password for each account reduces the risk of other accounts being compromised.

- **Avoid Personal Information**: Don't use easily obtainable information like your name, birthdate, or common words associated with you. This information is often the first choice for attackers.

- **Two-Factor Authentication (2FA)**: Whenever possible, enable 2FA for your accounts. This adds an additional layer of security by requiring a second form of verification besides just your password, such as a code sent to your phone or email address.

- **Avoid Common Passwords**: Avoid using easily guessable passwords like "password," "123456," or "qwerty." These are among the most common passwords and are easily targeted by attackers.

- **Avoid Patterns**: Don't use easily recognizable patterns on the keyboard, such as "12345" or "qwerty."

- **Consider Passphrases**: Instead of a random string of characters, consider using a passphrase—a combination of words or a sentence that is easy for you to remember but difficult for others to guess.

- **Check for Breaches**: Regularly check if your email or passwords have been involved in any data breaches. Websites like "Have I Been Pwned" can help you with this.

And beware of those silly little games on social media that ask you to list your dog's name, favorite colors, etc. These are used by hackers to trick you into giving up security questions for your bank, credit cards, and other websites you use to transact personal business. If you do play these games, just make sure none of your answers correlate to your security questions.

One more thing that should go without saying – change your passwords at least every 90 days. This may also be a hassle but is far better to keep them guessing than to have your passwords show up on the dark web and potentially expose you to a breach or worse.

Chapter Two: Safe Browsing Behavior

Bookmark sites you use all the time– don't just type the name into your browser

My husband Bert gets into trouble by entering his bank or credit card company name into the search bar and just hitting the first Google entry that comes up. Bad bad bad! Many hackers spoof sites such as well-known banks, so if you accidentally misspell the bank name, fake sites can come up. In all fairness to Google, if you type it correctly you will usually get the right entity. In any event, if you have secure sites that you go to regularly, bookmark them in a secure browser like Chrome or Firefox and click on the bookmark to access them so that you don't run that risk. Otherwise, you could land on a spoof site or site that deposits malicious programs like malware into your machine. Best case, it will slow you down. Worst case, it will infiltrate your machine and gain access to your information.

Be careful of "news" sites that are not syndicated or well-known
I reverse engineer Bert's computer every time he gets hacked, and another main source of malware he attracts is through fake or lesser-known news sites. If you click on a news headline from an advertisement, you run a huge risk of clicking on a malware laden site. Recently, many legitimate yet smaller news sites were infiltrated by hackers so that they download malware or tracking software onto every site visitor. If you want to look at news on your computer, it is best to stick to major, well-known sites and bookmark them. Visit them from the bookmark.

Don't click on aggregator/Ad sites for a consumer item that pops up on a news or other site
If you follow Clickbait (stories that pop up on the Yahoo or other home screen), sooner or later you will see photo ads at the bottom

11

of the page, or ads that promise the best prices for TVs, DVDs, or other specific items you may have been running searches around. These ads are almost always malware laden, and some even have fake merchandise advertised. It's best to stick to searching on reputable manufacturers sites like Home Depot, Best Buy, etc. And best not to fall for Clickbait in the first place, the stories usually run on and on forever so they can expose you to more ads and are a huge time waster. Better to pick up the phone and call a friend or relative or watch some TV if you really have time to kill.

Be careful when clicking links from ANYWHERE
Before you go all click-happy on a link, give it a hover. That means moving your mouse pointer over the link without clicking. Your computer will reveal the actual web address, and if it looks fishy or doesn't match what you were expecting, abort mission! It's like checking the peephole before opening the door. The bad guys can make the outward facing text look like a legitimate website, but when you use this trick, you will see that it is actually something completely different. Any time you do this and see something dramatically different from what is

displayed, it is time to stop. Do not click that link!

The same holds true for links to attachments originating from unknown senders in email. Do not click!

Don't blindly trust "Tiny URLs"
It's like unfolding a treasure map to make sure you're headed in the right direction. You know those short URLs that look like they were put through a shrink ray? While they're handy, they can also be a bit mysterious. If you get one, consider using a URL expander tool to reveal the full web address before taking the plunge. A good free one is CheckshortURL, it is browser based and easy to use. Just copy the tiny URL and put it in the window at this site.

If it sounds too good to be true, it is!
Some ads that come up in these Clickbait sites or social media offer items at an unheard-of low price. Although some are legitimate, some just want to get your credit card information so they can then charge a bunch of crazy stuff. Bert saw a chainsaw advertised for $12, jumped on it thinking he had a wonderful deal, and six weeks later he got just a very small chain for a tiny chainsaw in the mail. I did worse, even with

all my certs, I saw a teardrop trailer advertised for $160. I bit, and within 15 minutes I had to shut down the credit card as fraudulent charges were attempted on my account. I have not lived this one down, every time I give him the "Safety in Browsing" lecture he retorts with, "Oh yeah, what about the teardrop trailer?"
The lesson learned here is this – if it sounds like too good of a bargain, there is a catch somewhere. And this proves that even someone who holds a Cybersecurity certification can fall for the old "something for nothing" temptation.

Act on those annoying messages that tell you your browser is out of date!
The Internet browser people, like Google Chrome, Microsoft, and Firefox work hard to block loopholes that hackers can use to attack people like you. When they send you a message that your browser is out of date and you need to upgrade, all you need to do is follow the simple directions they send you. Does this stop all possible attacks? No, but you are safer than you were before you did the upgrade as at least some possible paths for hackers are blocked. This usually only takes a few minutes but being hacked and recovering from the hack can take hours or days. Patience is a virtue. One way to

think of it is this – updates are like booster shots for your devices!

It is also a good idea to have more than one browser on your computer, read further and you will find out why. I personally have Google Chrome, Firefox, and Safari installed.

Get a GOOD Antivirus and Antimalware Program

The old adage says an ounce of prevention is worth a pound of cure – having a good antivirus program can pay for itself. I personally use Malwarebytes; Forbes mentioned their solution was ranked best for real time protection. It has 24/7 phone, chat, and email support and is $3.75/month/device. I like it as it is easy to use, has a web based free "cleaning" utility for if you are hacked, has uninstall protection (yes, some viruses and malware can uninstall your AV programs), and doesn't slow your machine down to a crawl. Forbes lists Bitdefender as the overall best, and it is reasonably priced at $29.99/year. It also includes extras such as email security, coverage for 3 devices provided they are Windows PCs (a package that covers 5 devices that includes Mac is available for

$49.99), a file shredder, and privacy protection.

Be careful to check the reputation of any antivirus program you choose. Some that are advertised on the web are malware delivery programs and not true antivirus programs. Others are simply ineffective against modern threats.

Manage Your Privacy Settings
Dig into your device's settings and take control. You can decide who gets to see your information and who doesn't. From location services to app permissions, make sure you're comfortable with the level of access you're granting to different apps and features.

Remember, it's your device, and you're the boss!

What if You Are Surfing, and a Pop-Up Comes Up Telling You that You've Been Hacked?
A very common attack occurs where a popup appears, or your browser suddenly switches to a screen stating you are infected and must act immediately. It lists a phone

number to call that is supposedly from an IT service company. It may be accompanied by a robotic voice repeating repeatedly "Do not attempt to shut down your computer", or even whistles or sirens. Its entire purpose is to get you to pay money to turn the annoying sounds off.

Do NOT call and pay these people, they are not a real IT services firm! Also, don't just shut down your computer and ignore this threat, you need to cut it off before it migrates to other systems on your network. Shut down the browser, and open another browser window, then go to Malwarebytes free scanner and run it. If you have a Windows machine, some malware may shut down your keyboard as a deterrent to your fixing the problem. Hitting Function key 7 (F7) may fix this issue. Once you have run the program, make sure you follow the instructions on the screen to isolate or remove the malware.

The next thing to do is to reboot and look at your browsing history to see what you may have clicked on to get the malware in the first place. Then, go ask your nice relative (or kid next door) to put those URL addresses into the browser as blocked, so you can't visit them anymore. Also ask them to look at what is now set as your home screen; some malware will reset the home screen to the malicious site to keep you infected.

This type of hack happens to Bert a lot. I have the process down now. Sadly, it usually happened when I was in the middle of an important work project, with a time limit.

Chapter Three: Safe Social Media Behavior

Instagram, Facebook, LinkedIn, and many more social media sites are a great way to keep in touch with distant friends and relatives, but they can be fraught with dangers if not used correctly. Be careful when clicking on Facebook ads, it is best to hit the "Save for later" button under the ad and come back to it later to see if it has been flagged for any violations before patronizing the company that placed the ad. I have bought from ads on Facebook, so they are not all hackers lying in wait. But I always wait a few days first.

Other things to be aware of on social media are:

Act immediately if someone duplicates your profile on Facebook and sets themselves up as you.

Sometimes all they do is try to sell your friends crypto, but other times, they can trick your friends into giving them money, access your accounts by stealing your data, or worse, post obscene or profane content as if they were you. This can be very embarrassing.

If this happens to you, go to the fake or "cloned" account, click the "…" icon on the upper right, select Report Profile, and follow the instructions onscreen. Next, post on your real page that all friends receiving another friend request from you should ignore it, as you have been hacked.

Next, change your password not once, but twice so the person cannot follow the flow. This happens a lot and very rarely does a more serious hack result from it, but it can result in embarrassment and hassles.

Set up notifications for unauthorized logins

This way you will know if someone is accessing your account that is not you.

To do this on Facebook,
Open Facebook from your web browser.
Click the triangle in the upper right to open
the menu, then select "Settings & privacy."
Select "Settings."

Click Security and Login in the left-hand
column.

Scroll down to "Setting Up Extra Security."
Click "Edit" next to "Get alerts about
unrecognized activity."

Select "Get notifications" and then choose
an email address (or email addresses) to be
notified by email.

Click "Save Changes."

Two (or multi) Factor authentication
Most social media sites will also ask you if
you want to enable "Two-factor
authentication" (mentioned earlier, but
worth repeating). This takes extra time but
makes it much less likely you will be hacked
in the future. Many banks use this, and it
simply means that a code will be sent to
your mobile phone, email address, or other
device that you then need to enter in the site
you are accessing to prove it is really you. If
you don't have a smart phone, most

authenticators have an option where you can receive a phone call instead. If you have the choice to do this, it does add extra time and can be annoying, but is well-worth it for peace of mind and safety.

Social Media "Relationships"
A particularly insidious type of scam is where an unknown person "friends" you on Facebook, Instagram, or even LinkedIn and initiates a personal relationship. This is known as the "Romance Scam". These type scammers target lonely elderly people and builds rapport with them over time. Many victims of this scam even felt they were "in love" with the criminal. The criminal deepens the relationship, and then develops an urgent personal crisis that requires money from the victim. It starts small and escalates over time until some have lost their entire life savings, only to find the "person" they had a relationship with was not even real. Scammers invent whole fake personas, often based on social media mining to find what would attract their target. The real person behind the computer may be a far cry from the photos presented!

Preventing this type of attack means limiting or having no interactions with people you don't know on social media sites. If you don't know them, don't accept a contact request.

If you are lonely, join a book club or other social club in your community. Visit the library, or your local church. If you are not religious, find another hobby such as a gardening club or ham radio. There are many ways to meet real people in person, and not rely on the Internet which is prone to "cat-fishing" (the term for using someone else's photos and personal details to attract someone for a Romance scam).

Beware of Public WIFI
If you connect at an airport or coffee shop, be aware that some bad actors may spoof the sign on screen to trick you into connecting your computer, which will then be mined for your information. Most corporations require their employees to use a VPN or "virtual private network" when logging in on an unsecured, public WIFI network. If you do use these networks without protection, just make sure you don't conduct any personal business, like banking or paying with credit cards from these networks.

If you need to use these networks a lot (you are using group WIFI, or have very slow home WIFI), then it may be prudent to invest in a VPN service. The best that I know of for consumer use is NordVPN; it is $3.39/month for the standard package which includes antimalware software as well.

Keep your distance from unknown persons if using your computer remotely
Bad actors can look over your shoulder at a coffee shop or other public location and get key information such as your banking password and username. If you must conduct business over your computer, it is wise to invest in a privacy screen that blocks the view for anyone trying to peer at your screen from the side. They are very inexpensive and can be purchased at any computer shop. And they are less disruptive than a backwards elbow jab.

Look for signposts
The address, or URL, of a secure site always begins with https – where the S stands for secure. And a little padlock at the bottom of your browser indicates that the site uses encryption.

Enable Account Updates
Many vendors, such as banks or retail stores, offer updates to you if someone attempts to change your password. If a thief hacks into your account, enabling this feature will stop

him or her from changing your password and locking you out of your account while it is being "looted". Always check to see if this is available and use it if it is.

Chapter Four: The Importance of Up-to-Date Equipment

Every tradesman knows that owning good jobs is critical to doing the job right. Yet, many non techies or older adults try to get maximum mileage out of their computer by keeping it way past its prime. Older computers cannot take critical Operating Systems upgrades, which means most new security upgrades and patches cannot be installed. Old computers are a heyday for hackers and malware creators!

I find it is best to upgrade your laptop or PC every 18 months to three years (18 months for a PC, three years for a Mac). A good way to tell that you need to upgrade is when you can no longer install critical browser updates, or your Windows or Mac updates menu tells you that your Operating System is no longer supported. If you are in doubt, go ask the little shit down the street, he or she will know.

I recommend buying a premade system rather than trying to build you own, like the old days. Today's systems have cybersecurity software built in as middle ware which is tough to duplicate.
It is also critical to maintain key pieces of software, like Microsoft Office. Most major software provides today offer cloud-based versions – these are safer as they are maintained by the manufacturer and hosted in their cloud. I recommend going this way instead of trying to maintain individual software packages yourself. The days of floppy discs is long over.

I also recommend storing important files on the cloud. I personally use Google Drive which is secure and cost effective. There are lots of other choices such as Dropbox if you don't like Google. This way, if your computer does get hacked (or ruined in a disaster), you still have your critical files and information. Things like bank statements, tax returns, etc are also easier to access on your home computer than they are in the cloud. You can access Google Drive here – https://drive.google.com/drive/home

and just drag and drop files into the dashboard to store your files.

It should go without saying that a key program to keep up to date is your antivirus software.

Chapter Five: How Not to Fall for Phishing and Vishing Attacks

Another area that gets computer users into trouble is email. In "cybersecurity speak" a phishing attack is carried out when a malicious actor sends out an email (or a text) posing as a trusted company or person in order to gain critical information. An example is an email I received just a few days ago, telling me that my Amazon Prime membership had expired, and did I want to renew? Knowing what I know about phishing, I immediately logged into the Amazon site and checked to see if this was indeed true. As I thought, I still had nine months remaining on my Prime membership. Looking more closely at the email, I saw some characteristic typos and misspellings. These are always a strong clue that an email didn't originate from a reputable company. If I had clicked on the link to renew and entered my credit card information – the hackers would have then had a field day charging things to my account.

In today's AI (artificial intelligence) enhanced world, hackers can now just use ChatGPT (an artificial intelligence program) to correct the typical typos and errors associated with phishing attempts. This means we now need to be more careful than ever with responding to emails and clicking links.

Some more subtle things to look for that give away a phishing attack are:

- Hackers can use the Cyrillic or Slavic alphabet for certain characters, such as the letters a or e– to spoof an address so that it looks like the legitimate site. This looks very similar and can fool many – although it looks and acts the same to us, the computer treats it differently. An example is shown here (from https://www.linkedin.com/pulse/expl oring-intriguing-connection-cyrillic-alphabet-its-premshanal/)

citibank.com is not the same as
citibank.com
(the first one is correct, the second one
is from hackers)

The "a" in the later url is a cyrillic
alphabet.

- A sense of urgency – the hacker
  wants you to do something RIGHT
  NOW! The reason for this is they
  want you to act before thinking the
  situation through. Exploiting human
  emotions is part of their craft. Some
  ways this is done is by convincing
  their victim that their account has
  been hacked, and they need to
  change their password RIGHT
  AWAY. Once the victim has
  changed the password, the hacker
  now has it. Another way is by
  promising something free or heavily
  discounted that won't last. The
  criminal can also impersonate
  someone you know whom they say is

in trouble and needs you to send them money. In all these situations, it is critical to see the sense of urgency as a red flag instead of acting on the subject of the email.

- Claims that you have won the lottery, known as "Lottery Phishing". Check your numbers yourself at your local store, or via an approved app created by your State Lottery agency and don't fall for this one.

- Claims that a person with authority (your financial planner, former boss, doctor, etc.) needs your password or access to your computer, or money. If you get an email like this, pick up the phone and call the person directly. Most of the time they will confirm that it didn't come from them. A wrinkle on this is an email that claims to come from an IT firm or computer repair company. Likewise, they would not send you an unsolicited email out of the blue. This is another scam.

- Claims that a package delivery attempt was made, but postage was short. They just want you to pay some small amount, and they can deliver. If you enter a credit card, they now have your card information. This one happens a lot around the holidays.

- Claims that someone you know wants you to pick up a package for them or has left you some money in exchange for a task. Always check with the person first.

- An especially insidious type of attack is the "Fake Part Time Job" scam. Here, a fake interviewer emails you after seeing your resume on the web or applying for a part time job. They "interview" you and congratulate you for getting the job. But there is just one more step – they don't want you using your own computer equipment. They need you to use your own credit card to purchase up to $10K worth of new equipment for "maximum productivity". They take your credit card information, and days or weeks later, you discover there was no real job and no real equipment on its way. Always check the background

around any part time job you are
investigating.

- Emails can seem to come from your
friends but be spoofed. If they are
unexpected or look suspicious –
don't open any attachments that are
included. Many times, malware is
delivered via these types of
attachments.

What is a Vishing Attack?

"Vishing" is the same thing as a phishing
attack; the only difference is that the
scammer calls you instead of emailing you.
Make it a good practice to NEVER give out
bank account or credit card information over
the phone, unless you absolutely know you
are speaking to a valid representative of
your bank or other reputable institution.
Most reputable companies and agencies will
NEVER call you and ask for money.

A well-known scam of this type happens
when you receive a call with a Washington
DC area code that claims to be from the IRS.
They become very insistent (creating that
well-known sense of urgency) and claim that
you will be audited or worse if you don't
pay them and NOW. Never ever fall for this
one, reach out and call the IRS directly and

report that you have received a call like this so they can catch the perpetrators.

Another one claims to be your service provider with a notice that you have to pay a surcharge, or you will have your service shut off. Simply hang up, call the service provider, and confirm that this is a scam. They are usually quite happy to have people report these imposters so they can be shut down.

A particularly damaging type of attack is known as the "Grandparent" attack. A cybercriminal calls, claiming to either be a friend of a grandchild or an actual grandchild. These bad actors mine social media sites to find specific information about your grandchildren or other relatives and create a fake urgent scenario such as a car accident, hospitalization or needed bail to trick you into sending money. These bad actors are now using AI to almost exactly replicate the voice of your relative (called a "deep fake"), needing only a few second sample to make an almost indistinguishable copy. They can also spoof your relative's phone number, so it sounds and looks exactly like the call is real. If you receive an urgent call of this nature, don't act out of emotion. Take the time to hang up the phone and call the real person or someone close to them to confirm.

Engaging anti-spam call software like "Nomorobo" can help block vishing calls but is not foolproof. Keep your wits about you, and question everything.

It is also helpful to check consumer sites like the AARP Fraud Watch Network Scam-Tracking Map to see which scams are prevalent in your area.

An example (with the names changed) that happened in my county and was posted to this AARP site was as follows:

"My husband was called by a male identifying himself as our son Sam… he was crying hysterically and said I've been arrested for felonious assault here is my case number (and call my public defender Jay Wylie at xxx-xxx-xxxx please… as he is hysterically sobbing and says they are making me hang up I have a broken nose and split lip. I don't want to go to jail dad hurry … so my husband calls this "attorney" who I verified is an actual attorney in SF, he says the only way you can get your son released today (as we were terrified and frantic) is to have someone deliver $15000 in cash as it's a high bail amount Of 250000 but he is eligible for a pretrial diversion program that is $15,000 but refundable upon completion of the program. He answered the phone "public defender's office" I detected a slight East Indian accent, and he wasn't well spoken. This was Saturday July 9th at exactly 0827 on a private number saying it was our "son" this scammer called again at exactly 0843 from a xxx-xxx-xxxx mobile number stating he was Jay Wylie and told us "Sam got into a fight protecting a pregnant female who was being assaulted when the guy sucker punched him breaking his nose and splitting his lip, however "Sam" tackled him and the guy fell to the ground his head striking the cement and splitting open his head he is in critical condition" we do not know if he is going to make it and his girlfriend was pushed to the ground and complained of abdominal pains and was also sent by ambulance to the hospital. He said the judge signed an "order" stating" Sam" is eligible for the program because he has never been arrested and had no record so we would need $15000 in CASH. We asked if we could use a credit card. He said it would take days to process if we wanted "Sam" out today we would have to pay or send cash … he never gave any accounts to send to however he stated they had a "mobile clerk"

who could pick up the money and give us a receipt. Being a retired deputy sheriff, I knew at once this wasn't true and the "case # 0426771-A was not accurate as the year would be the first two numbers and this was not a court case number. Also, as a felony assault I told my husband that isn't accurate. The scammer said we needed to deliver $15000 in cash before noon to the courthouse in SF and there would be a clerk there able to process the bail and get Sam released. Thank God I saw red flags because when I called this "attorney" back the cell number was disconnected however this number and the lawyers name has been used on several occasions with a very real sounding familiar scam"

It is fortune that this woman had a law enforcement background, or this story may have had a much different ending

Another place to consult is the FTC (Federal Trade Commission), which has an excellent site detailing how to avoid these types of scams - https://consumer.ftc.gov/features/pass-it-on/impersonator-scams

PART II: Cell Phones, Credit Cards, and other Stuff

Scammers and hackers don't stop at telephones and computers in their attempts to separate you from your money (or identity). Your cell phone, credit cards, and even your WIFI enabled appliances such as Ring cameras and Nest thermostats can be targets.

One must remain vigilant in all areas, to be safe. Luckily, safety is easy once you know what you are up against. Bad actors can be teenagers or computer nerds in a small room with pizza and soda still, but today, hackers can also be radical nation-state actors (like Russians) who can use your device CPU power by aggregating many together to accelerate an attack on a more critical target, like US infrastructure. Russian, North Korean or other bad actor hacking teams also extort money to help finance wars.

How do you stay safe beyond the computer? Read on…

Chapter Six– Protecting Your Mobile Phone

Think your smart phone or mobile phone is safe? Think again. Hackers have found a haven in mobile smart phones, especially with the convenience of online banking and stored credit cards. I personally know people who have had their Venmo hacked into, and money taken.

Keeping your phone safe is a natural follow-on to keeping your computer safe. Spam texts are a major source of infections, don't click on any links that you don't recognize as from a legitimate retailer or website. If it looks at all suspicious, compare the address with the known, real link and see if any letters look different. Promptly delete all unwanted spam texts from your messaging.

If you log into any applications from your smart phone, make sure you use strong passwords and change them often. Enable facial recognition if offered by your phone, and use a strong, non-sequential PIN code as well.

If your phone starts loading slowly or acting funny, a virus or malware may be the culprit.

Just like on your computer, a good antivirus program is needed. I recommend the consumer version of Lookout, which is a company dedicated to mobile phone cybersafety. The cost is minimal and the peace of mind it provides is important. Other mobile antivirus software packages with good reviews and reasonable cost include Webroot, Bitdefender, and Trend Micro.

It is very important to only purchase software from officially sanctioned "stores" or marketplaces – like the App Store for iPhone. These applications have been carefully vetted to make sure they have no malware or bugs that can adversely affect your system.

Apple smartphones are inherently more secure than Android (author's opinion), and this is said to be partially because of the tight control Apple has over its App Store. I like Apple because I am used to it, and everyone I know who has an Android machine is always taking it to the shop.

Always keep your phone with you, some hackers can extract information from your phone if they access it while you visit the restroom or leave it on your desk. And never plug your phone into unknown charging stations or computers, as they can be rigged with malicious software that gains access to your device when connected.

If you haven't used an app for a while and aren't likely to ever use it – delete it. And make sure you check for updates for your apps on your phone just as you do on your computer – after all, your phone is just a smaller computer. These updates often contain security patches and block attack surfaces a bad guy could leverage to access your personal data.

In case the worst happens, and your phone is lost or stolen, make sure you have a feature enabled to allow you to remotely wipe it clean of all your personal data. Your carrier can help you enable this if you visit their store. This needs to be enabled ahead of time in order to be used.

If you have an iPhone – the "Find my iPhone" feature on iCloud is a great way to see if you have just misplaced it (as it shows up at your address), or if someone has actually lifted it. I had a phone stolen from the Mountain View High School library while I was coaching some speech and debate kids. "Find my iPhone" traced it to an apartment complex about 5 miles from the school. With this knowledge, I was able to report my phone stolen and remotely wipe it clean of all personal data.

Both Apple and Google offer step-by-step guides for wiping data off phones remotely once it becomes imperative to do so, for iPhone and Androids respectively. I strongly suggest you take this step if your phone is truly lost or stolen. Once again, this capability needs to be enabled in advance.

Secure Texts and Conversations

About once a month, I hear someone in a public place giving out their credit card or bank account numbers. This is very risky, as the wrong person may be overhearing. Be sure you are in a private location before giving out any critical data over the phone, if you must do so.

Texts can also be risky, and if you want to send secure texts or recordings, I suggest using either WhatsApp or Signal. Both offer end-to-end encrypted communications (encryption meaning encoded with a cipher that makes them harder to decode if your phone is lost or stolen). Signal may be the better choice as it is not owned by Facebook. Both allow you to create "disappearing" messages, which are deleted after a certain time limit.

Chapter Seven – Credit and ATM Cards

Credit card fraud can be especially annoying when you are traveling but can happen anytime and anywhere.

The easiest way that fraudsters get your credit card info is by standing too close to you in a check-out line or at the ATM. Make sure that anyone who is standing next to you moves before you reach for your card – if they are not perpetrating a fraud, they shouldn't mind being asked to move back a few steps!

Other avenues are by hacking into your computer (see earlier chapter), getting you to reveal your card info through vishing scams (see early chapter), by skimming card information from a gas station or merchant's card reader that has been altered, or by using an RFID reader when you are standing close to them.

To stay safe, first make sure that all the cards you own have $0 liability associated with fraudulent transactions. If you get hit, simply call the issuing bank and fill out a claim form.

Secondly, choose card providers that have a microchip embedded on your card. That makes it tougher, but not impossible, to skim your card for data.

RFID readers are used in crowded locations to skim info from people without ever touching them. Luckily, you can easily purchase RFID blocking wallets, purses, or card holders from places like Amazon that blocks the signal from getting through to the RFID skimmer. Bert had a credit card hit for $2,200 in the Salt Lake City airport. As it was a $0 liability card, he got it all back, but it took time and effort.

The virtual card – a new way to stay safe
A virtual card is a digital or online payment card that allows users to make purchases on the Internet without using their physical credit or debit cards. It is essentially a digital

representation of a traditional payment card and is designed to enhance security and privacy for online transactions. Here's how the concept of a virtual card works:

1. Digital Format:

   - Unlike physical cards made of plastic, a virtual card exists only in digital format. It comprises a set of card details such as the card number, expiration date, and a security code (CVV).

2. Issued by Financial Institutions:

   - Virtual cards are typically issued by banks, financial institutions, or online payment platforms. Users can obtain a virtual card through their bank's online banking platform or via specific financial apps.

3. Temporary or Disposable:

   - Some virtual cards are designed for one-time use or have a limited validity period. These are often referred to as disposable or temporary virtual cards. After the designated use or expiration date, the card becomes invalid, adding an extra layer of security.

4. Security Features:

   - Virtual cards often come with advanced security features. Since they are not physical, they are less susceptible to traditional card-related risks such as skimming or physical theft. Additionally, users may have the ability to freeze or deactivate a virtual card if it's not in use, providing greater control over their accounts.

5. Privacy Protection:

   - Virtual cards offer enhanced privacy for online transactions. Users can avoid exposing their primary credit or debit card details when making purchases online,

reducing the risk of
unauthorized access or fraud.

6. Convenience:

- Virtual cards are convenient
  for online shopping. Users
  can easily access their virtual
  card details through a
  banking app or online portal,
  eliminating the need to carry
  physical cards or manually
  enter card information for
  each transaction.

7. Budgeting and Control:

- Virtual cards can be a useful
  tool for budgeting and
  controlling spending. Users
  can set spending limits or
  allocate a specific amount to
  their virtual cards, helping
  them manage their online
  expenses more effectively.

8. Global Use:

- Virtual cards can often be
  used for international

transactions, just like physical cards. They may come with features such as currency conversion and the ability to make purchases from websites worldwide.

In short, if you want to take advantage of those wonderful Cyber Monday deals, it may be worthwhile to get a virtual card as a double layer of protection.

Apple Pay, Google Pay, and Venmo are also secure app-based ways to pay securely for goods or services. The only problem with Venmo is that everyone can see who you are paying, and for what. If you don't care that your kids see that you split expenses with Uncle Walter for bowling, then this is no issue.

Chapter Eight – WIFI Enabled "Stuff"

Alright, let's talk about why it's crucial to keep your home Internet safe, especially when you've got nifty gadgets like Ring cameras and Nest thermostats in the mix. I mean, we all love the convenience and cool features they bring to our homes, but they also open the door to potential cyber shenanigans.

Imagine this – someone gaining access to your Ring camera and peeking into your private space. Yikes, right? Well, that's why we need to chat about the importance of locking down our home Internet. These devices, as awesome as they are, can be a bit like unlocked doors for hackers if we're not careful.

Take Ring cameras and Nest devices, for instance. There have been cases where hackers got into the system and messed with people's privacy. Not cool. And it's usually because of weak passwords or outdated software. So, what can we do about it?

First things first, like we discussed in earlier chapters, let's set some rock-solid passwords. None of that "password123" business. Make them strong and unique for each device.

And another repeating theme, don't forget to update the software regularly – it's like giving your gadgets a little security boost.

Oh, and your WIFI network? Don't leave it wide open like an all-you-can-hack buffet. Slap on a strong password and maybe even some encryption to keep unwanted guests out. If you want to block some known bad actors and have a gateway provided by a service provider, call them and ask them to walk you (or the little shit next door) through how to strengthen your firewall settings.

Here's a nifty trick – turn on two-factor authentication. It's like having a bouncer at the digital entrance, making sure only you get VIP access. We talked about this briefly earlier, but it bears repeating as it is a great tool for your home Internet as well.

So, the bottom line: keeping your home Internet safe is not just about passwords and software updates; it's about protecting your personal space.

Chapter Nine – Yep, Old Fashioned Stuff Can be Scam Fodder Too

Todays' scammers are more sophisticated than ever before. What used to be safe, is no longer something that can be trusted. The first thing to be aware of, is…

Your mail

The US mail used to be the most secure thing going, but mail thieves are now everywhere. It is now safer to make a payment over the web with a virtual card than it is to mail a check – as mail thieves can easily break into the mailbox and steal your letter. Once they do, they can open your envelope, pull out your check, and get your address, account number, and routing number. A good identity thief can do lots with just that information!

If you must mail checks, make sure you enclose them in paper or another blocking wrapper so that thieves cannot easily identify the mailing as containing a check. At least make it tougher for the bad guys. Do the same if you are sending in a mailer that includes your credit card information. Most companies don't use those mailers anymore, because of mail theft. But there are a few who still do. If there is another way to pay, I suggest taking it.

Likewise, I recommend getting your bank, credit card, and investment account statements online. One of the easiest ways for a thief to steal your identity is stealing your mail. Once a crook has your card numbers and account numbers, he or she can use this information to impersonate you for financial gain and other, more insidious reasons (see Chapter Ten)

If you dispose of old mail, make sure that you run it through a shredder if it contains any personally identifiable information. Crooks go through your trash also.

Cut up old credit cards and ATM cards before disposing of them, as thieves do sort through trash for anything they can sell.

If you go out of town on vacation, a good practice is to have your mail held at the post office.

Picking up your mail as soon as it arrives and not letting it sit in the box is also a good practice.

Your wallet

If you lose your purse or wallet, common wisdom dictates that you immediately call and cancel your credit cards. You also need to notify your bank and possibly the passport agency and DMV (Department of Motor Vehicles) to protect your identity.

Buying or selling from Craigslist, local papers, or Facebook Messenger
Bargains abound when you take the time to search classified ads, but so do scammers, identity thieves, and other crooks.

When meeting someone to exchange money, goods or services from a classified ad – be sure to always bring someone else with you. That way, if things are really a set up for a robbery, you have someone who can run and call the authorities.

Be very vary of personal checks, and by no means should you ever take a cashier's check. There is a known cashier's check forgery scam where the perpetrators send you a fake check in the mail for a large ticket item and expect you to ship the item before the check has cleared. When the check bounces, you no longer have your high-ticket item to sell and have nothing to show for it.

Yet another classifieds scam involves selling stolen merchandise. The seller claims to be the original owner. If you sense something fishy, walk away. You can be caught holding the bag and prosecuted instead of the real thief!

Chapter Ten – Identity Theft and How to Prevent It

Identity theft can happen to anyone and is unfortunately becoming quite common. Hackers can get your personal information through many of the ways detailed in earlier chapters – but the incredible number of data breaches we hear about in the news every day is something we can't control.

If you receive a notice that you have been involved in a data breach, it is time to start being vigilant. Pay careful attention to your bank and credit card statements, and your credit report. A credit report will show any new accounts that may have been opened in your name without your permission.

A thief who gets your information may also use it to get unauthorized medical services. This means you also need to monitor your medical insurance statements to make sure there is nothing unknown or that doesn't apply to you.

Criminals can steal your information, file a change of address form, and file a tax return as if they were you in order to get your refund. If you get a rejection of your tax return with the explanation that it has already been filed, it is time to suspect identity theft.

Identity criminals can also give your data if arrested – and this can cause you issues for many years if not addressed.

Passport numbers or actual passports are especially valuable to traffickers as they can get their victims into the United States using a forged version of your passport, assuming your identity.

Identity Theft Insurance
One way you can protect yourself against the negative impact of identity theft is to purchase identity theft insurance. In 2022, the FTC received 1.1 million complaints about identity theft, with most being some form of credit card fraud.

Identity theft insurance cannot fully prevent fraud – nor does it cover any monies stolen by the crooks. Then, you may ask, what good is it?

If your identity is stolen, recovery can be a giant headache. Identity insurance will cover legal fees, registered or certified mail fees, lost wages due to the time needed for recovery, notary fees related to resolving the theft, child, spousal or elder care needed while you are resolving the theft, and any phone bills. Some also cover access to identity repair experts, credit bureau monitoring, full family coverage, and scanning to see if your information is on the "dark web".

What is this ominous thing known as the "dark web"? It's called "dark" as it is intentionally hidden, requiring a specialized browser to view. Criminals use it for sex trafficking, illicit drug deals, weapons deals, trading of illegal pornography and all sorts of nasty things, not the least of which is trading stolen identities. If you are notified that an email or password has been found on the "dark web", it is time to get a stronger and better password.

How do you choose an Identity Theft service? It depends on how many resources you have at risk and what your overall exposure is. The two most common coverages are $500K and $1M – if your resources are not extensive, you may not need the full $1M coverage.

Always investigate any service carefully before making a purchase. A great source of trustworthy reviews is Forbes magazine, which lists these as the best Identity Theft insurance services:

- **Best overall:** IdentityForce®
- **Runner-up:** PrivacyGuard™
- **Best for credit monitoring:** Experian IdentityWorks℠
- **Best for identity theft insurance:** Identity Guard
- **Best for computer and device protection:** LifeLock®

The services inclusive of credit monitoring can help you spot any fraud early. The earlier you detect identity theft, the easier it is to resolve.

These policies range from $0 (Experian has a free very basic version that offers protection and notification, but no insurance coverage) to $40/month based on the overall package offered.

Always read the fine print for any service you choose, to make sure there are no "gotchas" or caveats that could keep you from the help you need should the unthinkable happen.

To report identity theft, go to identitytheft.gov and follow the instructions there. Once again, immediate action is best. Identity theft is like an oil spill – it needs cleaned up fast!

Epilogue/Conclusion

Friends, seniors, and "non-techies"; we have come to the end of our journey through staying safe in this digital age and finished our mission to arm you with the savvy skills needed to own your cybersecurity game. We've covered everything from crafting unbreakable passwords to outsmarting those tricky online scams.

Each chapter was created to be like a chat with a tech-savvy friend (or the little shit next door, without the attitude), giving you down-to-earth tips to keep your online adventures safe and sound.

We dove into securing your gadgets, spilled the tea on social media risks, and kept you in the loop about the latest cyber mischief. Our goal was to make this whole cybersecurity thing less of a head-scratcher and more of a breeze for our awesome readers.

And there you have it, the grand finale of our "Cybersafe Seniors and Non-Techies" journey! We've shouted from the digital rooftops that you, yes YOU, can own this online world. By picking up the habits and tricks we've shared, you're not just surfing the web; you're doing it with a superhero cape of cyber safety.

In this wild web of connections, age is just a number, and cybersecurity is for everyone. As you wave goodbye, carry these cyber-savvy tools with you. Let them be your trusty sidekick, ensuring that every online adventure is not just fun but safe too. Stay savvy, stay secure, and keep rocking that cyber confidence!

Stay alert, stay aware, and stay safe!

Bibliography

1. Sunny Skyz. (n.d.). ID10T Error Joke. Retrieved from https://www.sunnyskyz.com/funny-jokes/1/ID-ten-T-error

2. OpenAI. (n.d.). ChatGPT 3.5. Retrieved from https://www.openai.com

3. HostHelp.net. (n.d.). What Websites have the Most Viruses. Retrieved from https://www.hosthelp.net/what-websites-have-the-most-viruses/

4. Forbes Advisor. (2024). 10 Best Antivirus Software (January 2024). Retrieved from https://www.forbes.com/advisor/business/software/best-antivirus-software/

5. Techlicious. (n.d.). What is Facebook Account Cloning and What Can You Do About it? Retrieved from https://www.techlicious.com/tip/facebook-account-cloning/

6. Anton, P. C. (n.d.). Exploring the Intriguing Connection: The Cyrillic Alphabet and its Utilization by

Hackers. Retrieved from
https://www.linkedin.com/pulse/exploring-intriguing-connection-cyrillic-alphabet-its-premshanal/

7. Federal Communications Commission (FCC). (n.d.). 'Grandparent' Scams Get More Sophisticated. Retrieved from https://www.fcc.gov/grandparent-scams-get-more-sophisticated

8. AARP. (n.d.). Scam-Tracking Map. Retrieved from https://www.aarp.org/money/scams-fraud/tracking-map/

9. Federal Trade Commission (FTC). (n.d.). Impersonator Scams. Retrieved from https://consumer.ftc.gov/features/pass-it-on/impersonator-scams

10. Identiy Fraud Cost Consumers $16.9B in 2019 – Here's How Identity Theft Insurance Can Help. Retrieved from https://www.cnbc.com/select/id-theft-insurance/

11. What is Identity Theft Insurance? Retrieved from https://www.experian.com/blogs/as

k-experian/what-is-identity-theft-insurance/
12. Federal Trade Commission - https://www.identitytheft.gov/#/
13. How to Prevent Getting Hacked Retrieved from https://www.wired.com/story/how-to-prevent-getting-hacked/

Acknowledgements

Cover Art is by Stockimg.AI, Author photography by Bert Johnson, One Instant in Time Photography

Thank you to Bert Johnson whose experiences inspired this book (although I complained at the time), and to the many tech companies that forced me to stay on top of my computer skills AND conducted cybersecurity safety trainings. Thank you also to the I2C and all the wonderful updates they have for our craft of cybersecurity.

About the Author

With nearly four decades of experience, **Brenda Johnson** has navigated the dynamic landscape of high-tech companies, including VMware, Cisco Systems, and the cybersecurity startup Carbon Black. Holding the esteemed CISSP (Certified Information Security Systems Professional) certification, she channels her passion into the cybersecurity domain, viewing it as a means to combat today's formidable cyber threats.

Beyond her professional pursuits, Brenda is a trumpet player and member of the Sacramento big band "The Swingmasters."

An enthusiastic reader of Science Fiction, she also engages in ham radio as a hobby and is an active member of the El Dorado County Amateur Radio club and El Dorado County Emergency Radio Services. She resides in both Pollock Pines, California and Sacramento, California with her husband Bert, two half Jack Russell half Chihuahuas, and three cats.

Follow Brenda on Linked in at
https://www.linkedin.com/in/brendajohn1/